I0109034

Leaning Toward Whole

OTHER BOOKS BY M. D. FRIEDMAN

The Body of the Mind

From Here to Here

Nothing Else Matters

Where We Reach

Leaning Toward Whole

by M. D. Friedman

Liquid Light Press
Premium Chapbook First Edition

Copyright © 2011 by M. D. Friedman

ISBN: 978-0-9836063-0-7

All rights reserved. Except for brief passages quoted in
newspaper, magazine, radio, television or online reviews, no
part of this book may be reproduced in any form or by any
means, electronic or mechanical, including photocopying,
scanning and recording, or by information storage or retrieval
systems, without permission in writing from the Author.

Liquid Light Press

poetry that speaks to the heart

www.liquidlightpress.com

Cover Art
Mother's Whispers by M. D. Friedman
www.mdfriedman.com
Copyright © 2009 by M. D. Friedman

Leaning Toward Whole

in memory of
Eleanor Friedman
1921- 2007

Leaning Toward Whole

Bristling sunlight
breaks the quiet
morning. Frost sublimes
without a whimper.

Everything sheds
its own luminance,
leans like shadow
toward the hole

into the center
of the bright storm.
Our hearts hum
their resonant
invitation.

A vibrant
eye of light
opens the more intently
we listen, the more
gracefully we breathe.

Poets Two

In the long slide down a smooth sheer rock wall

two poets hang, dark stone flush to their backs.

The sun sears their flesh raw, once light now black.

Heels dug into holes to retard their fall,

they chant the wonder of being here at all.

Their words fill us with what we lack;

the river below floods earth's crack.

Their songs the longings quench of our hearts' call.

Sacred yearning drags us in once again.

It's as if poetry that from them fell

somehow held them above the ghouls of hell.

Their wild rhymes so confused gravity's sin.

The birds that sing so having sung fly on.

We all fall into song until we're gone.

Light Returns

The beasts of light
return to my window,
one by one they swirl down
from the hunched night
falling out of the stars
like solstice spangle.

They lock their wiry feet
on thin winter branches
as black as the land of their birth.
No, I am not dying. These are not angels.
Like a great Lazy Susan, this world
and the other have not changed places.

They are a wild
flaming flock of fluttering hundreds.
The creatures of light
gather and settle.
Each understands its place
in the night and how to hold on.

All at once they burst open
with a single luminous chorus of color.
They throw their brilliance
to the clouds, flood
the shadowed false dawn
with throbbing cadmium and crimson.

It is as if my heart, too, explodes,
no longer able to contain my blood
suddenly transfigured
into pulsing scarlet light.
No, I am not dead. The buzz
of my breath still drones within me.

I love the long quiet
of this moment
before they erupt again,
flare with a final burst
of iridescent grandeur
into the flickering blood lit sky.

Incarnate

We glide with the light that fires the dawn.

We wander and roam our crooked way home.

It seems not far from when we began

That the fat of our meat falls from our bone.

Stripped of all sense, blood and flesh,

No reason to eat the eye that's left.

We fly toward the hum our bodies formed from.

Our final and first gasp, forever alone.

What has been is yet to become.

I am you and you are me.

We'll do this all again

Until we learn to see.

The Great Clock

The few trees left
bear fruit of flame that smudge their muddy bark.
There is wisdom in the glowing pomegranates
that whirl hissing to the ground like molten tears.
There is peace in the breathing
blue leaves of sky, a stormy beauty
in the dirty tricks of cloud.

When fall goes, there is nothing left.
Lonely ashen spikes
branch into simple nonexistence,
await the quenching hush
of winter's white.

The people in the town
peep out through their shutters.
They wait still, breathless, rolling their big eyes
like bright apples along the slits of shade.
Outside, a single mottled arm directs the traffic of the wind,
guides the confused, gritty air
like a conductor shaping Shostakovich.

There is a long, smooth bridge with no one on it.
It opens into the dream, into the shadowed hills
beyond the river of birdsong — a hand of black glass
that reaches into the place we know is there
but can never see when we look for it.

So suddenly spring, the sun
on the bright horizon is falling in on itself,
leaving a magenta dimpled swirl
in the red brick dawn,
like a shimmering pink dust devil
trailing a dazzling wake of metallic feathers,
as if a wild, giant peacock molted as it climbed the sky.

The people flood out,
swelling the streets with human whirlpools,
swinging each other around in ever changing pairs,
an endless chain of arms locking and unlocking,
carelessly flinging each other into another.

A song, more a clamor,
rises from the crowd like smoke.
The rhythm, a hollow pulse,
throbs from the tower of the broken church
in the dead center of the square.
The great clock still tick ticks there
as incessant and monotonous as their own hearts.

The old church catches fire but no one seems to care.
New people come into town from across the bridge,
spiraling out of the darkness with no bodies at first.
No one anywhere has a face anyway, only one red flame
eye smiling or snarling or opening like a hungry mouth.

The clock tower, now a black skeleton,
a charcoal sketch of itself,
collapses with a heaving sigh,
a litany of ash, a chiming of embers.
One at a time the people go home,
back to their shuttered houses,
back to their own dark beginnings.

Raven's Treat

Raven comes to my garden
in the cool green evening
head cocked and shiny,
feet wired to strawed earth.

He sips flat brown beer
from a muddy slug trap,
fishes out with scissored beak
those slugs that slid in last night.

A fine fellow always full of fancy,
he throws his sharp head back,
letting them slime down
his throat like raw oysters.

Raven tells me how tasty slugs are
slowly marinated like this
in barley malt
and warm sunshine,

and laughs how they are,
in fact, fat, juicy reincarnated
bar flies that couldn't
resist "just one more beer."

Crop full, he dances boisterously,
a shadow on golden straw,
crackling and cawing,
spitting out dark haiku like tobacco,

cackling each one twice, each one twice,
his obsidian
eyes splash rivulets of black
dimming the raw dusk.

The Lost River

shiny shiny
go now
hungry
thirsty
swallowing
being swallowed
this is it
go now
into the deep
into the dark hole
into thundering quiet
dream now
sleep into the foil
seep onto the coals
sizzling silver
glowing fish
swim within the fire
swim through dull ash
the taste of smoke
leap into the brilliant fall
over rounded rock
over frothing rivulets
into the shining pools
into the shining pool
salty with spawn and sunlight
steaming with life

drink deeply your own blood
eat your fill
go now fisherman
caught in flesh
go now fish
go

In Search of the Planetary Penis

As a young virgin
she leaped the flames naked
singeing herself down to precious skin.

Since then no mere man has been enough.
The earth needs her now,
her whirling dance, her rituals of love.

The first voice of clarity
cries from her heart,
rises in chants and ravings.

She craves the rippling muscles of the waves,
lives to heal wounds of sharp steel and cement,
quiet the screams of forest leveled by bulldozer.

She has been freed from the confusion of many,
those who always want more
forever busy going somewhere else.

She feels alone but not lonely,
one woman to speak for all that is human,
to soothe the dry bark of vanishing wolf,

satisfy the moans of eroding cliff,
change the world one poem at a time.
A simple child of moonlight, so alive, a shining

apparition in the long night of the American dream,
her single quest, to quell the rising tower of our babble,
to loosen our choking spasm of greed.

Spring Love Poem

*Not only the thirsty seeks the water
but the water seeks the thirsty as well. – Rumi*

I reach with my eyes
into the pool of you,
the ripples of our yearning
splinter our reflection.

Here in the lotus of breath,
whirls the stars and moon
in sensual dance.
Immersed in fragrant emersion,

we are closer than touch.
The air you breathe,
I b r e a t h e,
closer than the blood that fills our hearts.

I have known this forever.
I remember each time
I am with you,
I have known forever

that somehow we will
always be together.
I have lived for this
when nothing else made sense.

Li Po Returns to His Lover in the Night

In honor of the Poet Immortal who drowned
trying to embrace the moon's reflection in a river.

It is magical indeed
how I fell without suffering
into the watered moon
light, how I still
breathe with the wind.

Can you hear me
rattling the leaves
over your head,
moaning (like your new lover)
against the dark earth?

Do you feel it now? My vague
hand sweeps the smooth
hair from your glistening eyes
as gently as the languid
lotus petal falls from the flower

behind your ear, swirls against
the silken robes
crumbled at your feet.
Though tonight you find me in every
sigh, in every pale shadow,

tomorrow do not bemoan
my moving on. For with each breath
I come and go. Like moon
laden tears of dew, I vanish
in a blaze of morning light.

Never Ask a Poet Directions

~ for Jared Smith

To start with
don't walk too fast.
It is best to lean
into each step
so as to feel

the ground move you.
Circle to your left
around the pitched arm
of the barren tree that twists
toward the fired sky.

Don't look up.
This way you may
enjoy the exquisite
pain of your passing
again and again.

It might go better yet
to model Alice
and make yourself
very, very small.
It may take most of your life

just to cross the footprint
of the mother raccoon,
but do not look back
upon a path glittered with regret,
lest you fall like tears

from the eye
of your own making.
When you find that place
where her sharp claws
have punctured the dark loam,

stop and rest.
You may even need to sleep
before you go in.
Most do.
You will know

when you are ready.
The warm heave
of your breath
will waken you. Of course,
it is always dark.

When what little light there is
films the rounded stone like milky dew,
it will be time to move again.
Follow the ragged ravine
that winds to your right

as if you were water.
Do not fixate
on the wiggle
of your falling.
Remember,

there is nowhere
to go but down.
As you catch the hang of it,
you will begin to roar.
The clamor of everyone

you have ever known
will be echoing
vociferously inside you.
A few lusty
cries will rise

from this surge of word
only to resubmerge
just as they start
to make sense.
You will not be missed,

though it will seem
like forever
you are gone.
Eventually,
things settle down.

You become as flat
and smooth as
a velvet pool
in the moonlight.
There is nothing left

but yourself
as far as
you can see
and still you
will expand.

You will know
when you arrive
because it is like
you have never left.
Ask a poet

directions, only
when you realize
you have
no place
left to go.

Do Not Run From Your Poet Self

~ for Billy Collins

do not fear your poet self
when you discover him under your lifeboat hiding
do not punish him like a pathetic stow away

what he has to say
will not throw you overboard
he is you as much as you are he

no matter what he says
it will not hurt for long
just a pinch

like a doctor giving a shot
his words will heal you
in the end

he will not preserve your pain
only hold it up shining to the night
like a broken sextant

after a while you will be left
at peace and adrift
in a small boat all your own

with a golden sail full of desire
you will have clean water and food for your mind
and a map if you are ever lost again

never call it mutiny or torture the words
that swirl in his wake as he slips
beneath the waves hoarse from screaming

for it was he who sang you back to life
when you bobbed and wretched across the lonely sea
and you will need his help again

Know Where to Go Crazy

He is going nowhere, deliberately. – Elizabeth Robinson

I've been here before,
where the rain cuts through like shard glass
drives me deep into the mouth of fog,

frozen, frosted with flakes of salt.
This is nowhere to go crazy.
When I move again, I return to somewhere,

anywhere there is something.
I'm done with that circle of tears
where dark fears fall from a lightening cracked sky.

It's over. The only way out is in.
There is nothing to say except it's time to leave.
There's nowhere to go, so I'm off.

It might as well be a picnic,
with this frayed tablecloth
I keep in my back pocket to blow my nose.

There is nothing to take. A bleeding
wafer of heart between two loaves
of breath is all I need.

I linger in the ghosted meadow.
My soul in its blue bottle
stirs the rocks to breathe.

I want only to blaze my own way,
to climb my high green hill
where each star shines alone.

Sure, I'll miss the warmth of the crowd,
the clap of strangers bumping into me,
broken music takes me now, ears stuffed to the brain.

No time to stay. No reason for more of the sane.
My screams fall like paper. I leave what is left
for another to write.

No desire for the ashes of this burning world.
My breath fogs my glasses.
In a dark way, I am filled with light.

I am ready. I've had no sleep for weeks.
My eyes open from looking inward.
I have sharpened my teeth.

Inside, it never changes. Every way I turn
leads back. I awake ever closer to sleep.
The edge of my dream cracks with beauty.

I wish I could take you. Here in the middle
of nowhere, there is so much to share.
The silence is shattering. It is a miracle just to be alive.

Bedside Manner

~ upon the passing of my mother

The dying have no sense
of when. Everything is
was, each breath,
a terrible wind.

The light of those they love
gathers like a tempestuous mob
shaking smoking torches
outside the window,

blazes like a hidden sun,
flooding the river of glass
with the searing certainty
of inevitable dawn.

The dying always walk
the other way, forgetting
all paths lead back, like breathing,
the way in is the way out.

I was there when she tumbled
like a flaming magnolia
down the long well of her mind.
I felt the exquisite weightlessness,
then her fear. What happens

at the bottom? She clenched
my hand in hers in mine in hers.
Although she was ashen as a tear of dust,
hollow as the peeled skin of snake,

I asked her if she remembered
the time in temple when her just
fallen father's thick veined hand
squeezed hers squeezing mine.

He came to tell you
it's all right. She remembers
to let go. Falls forever.
Nothing is more beautiful.

The Barn

        year after year
the red barn
lodged in twilight snowcaps
fades to grey   leaves
    scarlet   molt into black earth

        everything shimmers in
    familiar light

        one short season ago this
field erupted pulsing red   violet
whirred like an electric humming bird
-- splinters of bees burst through molten green
    into bloom after flaming bloom

        on my way home
    i find myself
                    leaving
myself   finding myself
    gone

        graceful in decay
barn wood
wormed with sunset
a bright urgency
    fires my return

an old board
hoards its shadow
swallows hard
against the twisting wind

Never Night

only the sun unacquainted
with darkness burns in my core

slice after slice flames
off the bright globe of breath

inside the in
finite instant

my heart spins
on the head of a pin

words shed from the swelling calm i
fall into more than can be said

M. D. Friedman is a poet, teacher, musician,

photographer, digital artist and web designer from

Lafayette, Colorado. Thousands of copies of his first four

books have been enjoyed by readers throughout the world.

His audio poem, "A Good Dog," was the overall winner of

the Book Habit & New Zealand Poetry Society 2008 Poetry

Contest. His new genre, digital poetry, represents the

artistic fusion of all his creative pursuits at once. He is the

founder of the popular Internet Poets' Cooperative website

which features over 20 free volumes of e-books from poets

around the world, over 1000 audio recordings of dozens of

Colorado poets reading their own work and over 40 videos

from the Poets' Co-op TV Show. His personal web site,

www.mdfriedman.com, offers access to all of M. D.

Friedman's creative ventures.

Acknowledgements:

Bedside Manner, was the second place winner in the free verse category of the Columbine Poets of Colorado 2009 Award.

Do Not Run From Your Poet Self & *Know Where to Go Crazy* were previously published online by Jane Crown in <u>Heavy Bear</u>.

Know Where to Go Crazy in its two voice version is available as a digital poem (in video format) at *www.mdfrieman.com* and on iTunes.

The following poems have previously appeared in anthologies published by Green Fuse Poetic Arts:

> *Li Po Returns to His Lover in the Night* -- <u>IMPROV 2008</u>
>
> *Poets Two* -- <u>BEYOND PLUTO</u> (2008)
>
> *Leaning Toward Whole* -- <u>BEYOND PLUTO</u> (2008)
>
> *The Lost River* -- <u>IMPROV 2007</u>
>
> *In Search of the Planetary Penis* -- <u>IMPROV 2007</u>

Back cover photo by Tera Seville (*www.myspace.com/photosbytera*)

www.ingramcontent.com/pod-product-compliance
Lightning Source LLC
Chambersburg PA
CBHW021915040426
42447CB00007B/872